The Really **Wild Life** of **Insects**™

ORCHID MANTISES

ANDREW HIPP

The Rosen Publishing Group's
PowerKids Press™
New York

For my wife, Rachel, who wanted to catch me a praying mantis in a jar.
Thank you for this good life of ours.

Published in 2003 by The Rosen Publishing Group, Inc.
29 East 21st Street, New York, NY 10010

First Edition

Editor: Gillian Houghton
Book Design: Mike Donnellan, Michael de Guzman

Photo Credits: Cover © Michael Fogden/Animals Animals; back cover, pp. 4, 7, 12, 15, 15 (inset), pp. 19, 20 © Robert & Linda Mitchell; p. 7 (inset) © James P. Rowan; p. 8 © Arnold Newman/Peter Arnold, Inc.; p. 11 © Michael & Patricia Fogden/CORBIS; pp. 16, 16 (inset) © Dwight Kuhn.

Hipp, Andrew.
Orchid mantises / by Andrew Hipp.—1st ed.
    p. cm. — (The really wild life of insects)
Summary: Describes the physical characteristics, behavior, life cycle, protective devices, and relatives of the orchid mantis.
Includes bibliographical references (p.   ).
  ISBN 0-8239-6239-3 (lib. bdg.)
1. Orchid mantis—Juvenile literature. [1. Orchid mantis.] I. Title.
  QL505.9.H94 H56 2003
  595.7'27—dc21
                                                    2001004847

Manufactured in the United States of America

CONTENTS

FUN FACTS

ORCHID MANTISES OFTEN HUNT FROM THE SENDUDOK, A FLOWERING SHRUB COMMON IN SOUTHEAST ASIA.

KANCHONG, THE ORCHID MANTIS

In the jungles of Southeast Asia lives a fierce predator, an animal that hunts other animals for food. Just from 2 to 3 inches (5–8 cm) long, it looks much like a flower. It has either pink or white skin, and its rear legs have broad, petal-like wings. With its strong, spined front legs, it can crush prey twice its size. The Malaysian people call it the Kanchong. Others call this insect an orchid mantis. The orchid mantis hides in flowers, waiting for prey. When a fly passes by, the mantid's front legs dart out. The mantis grabs the fly and bites through the back of its neck, killing it instantly. Then the beautiful Kanchong eats its prey.

This adult male orchid mantis blends into his surroundings in Pahang, Malaysia.

AN ORDER OF HUNTERS

The orchid mantis is one of about 1,800 praying mantid **species**. Most mantids, including the orchid mantis, live in the **tropics**. Others live in cooler places, such as **Eurasia** and North America. All mantids have triangular-shaped heads with two large **compound eyes** and three **ocelli**, or simple eyes. Unlike most insects, they can turn their heads freely to watch their prey. Mantids also have **raptorial** front legs, which they fold in front of themselves while waiting for prey. They look like they are praying. This behavior gives mantids their name. The name "Mantid" and the name of the mantis **order**, Mantodea, come from the Greek word for **prophet**.

Mantids do not stalk. Instead they wait for their prey with their forelegs folded, ready to strike at anything that passes by.

FUN FACTS

MANTIDS ARE BELIEVABLE LEAF, FLOWER, AND BARK MIMICS, BECAUSE THEY ARE ABLE TO SIT VERY STILL AS THEIR PREY APPROACHES.

Mantids usually hunt insects, but they also have been known to attack small mice and birds. They wait for their prey on flowers, in grasses, or on tree branches. Most adult mantids are very well **camouflaged**. Many have **cryptic** coloring, which is coloring that helps them disappear into their surroundings. A mantid might be green, like grass, or as brown as tree branches and dead leaves. Some mantids, including the orchid mantis, are **mimics**. This means that they look and act like something other than what they are. Some mantis species look and act like flowers, twigs, bark, or dead leaves.

Mantids are well suited to their surroundings. A bright green mantid blends in with nearby leaves.

MASTERFUL MIMICRY

Besides its coloring the orchid mantis has unusual markings that complete its disguise. There is a black spot on the tip of its **abdomen**. From just a few feet away, the spot looks like a fly resting on a flower. Other flies are attracted to the spot and land near it, making themselves easy prey for the mantis. Across the mantid's **thorax** runs a thin, green stripe. It divides the head and the thorax from the abdomen. This stripe helps the mantis hide from predators and prey. The orchid mantis is larger than any one flower petal. The stripe makes the orchid mantis look like two small petals instead of one large petal.

Petal-like structures on an orchid mantis' hind legs add to the insect's disguise, but they make it hard to move quickly.

FUN FACTS

THE SLOW SWAYING OF AN ORCHID MANTIS MIGHT MAKE IT APPEAR TO BE A PETAL MOVING IN THE WIND.

Adult mantids have excellent eyesight. Their large compound eyes are set far apart from each other. The distance between its eyes enables a mantid to tell how far away its prey is and to strike quickly. While waiting for prey a mantid sways gently back and forth. By measuring how much its prey appears to move, the mantid can tell how far away it is. A mantid also has a long, skinny ear on the underside of its thorax that allows it to hear the high-pitched squeaks and chirps of bats, which are dangerous predators. The combination of camouflage and keen senses keeps mantids well fed and safe from their predators.

A mantid's senses of sight and of sound will help it to find food and to avoid becoming a bat's next meal.

MANTID MATING

A male mantid's most dangerous predator might be his mate. An orchid mantid female is twice as long as her mate, because she must have both the energy to produce eggs and an abdomen large enough to hold them. She will not hesitate to attack a male that approaches her carelessly.

A male mantid might see his mate from a distance, or he might sense **pheromones** that the female gives off. He watches her from a safe distance, too far away for her to strike. Then he jumps onto her, and the mantids mate. After mating, the male usually runs or flies away to avoid becoming his mate's next meal.

Sometimes a female orchid mantis (right) *will bite off the head of her much smaller mate* (inset) *while they are mating.*

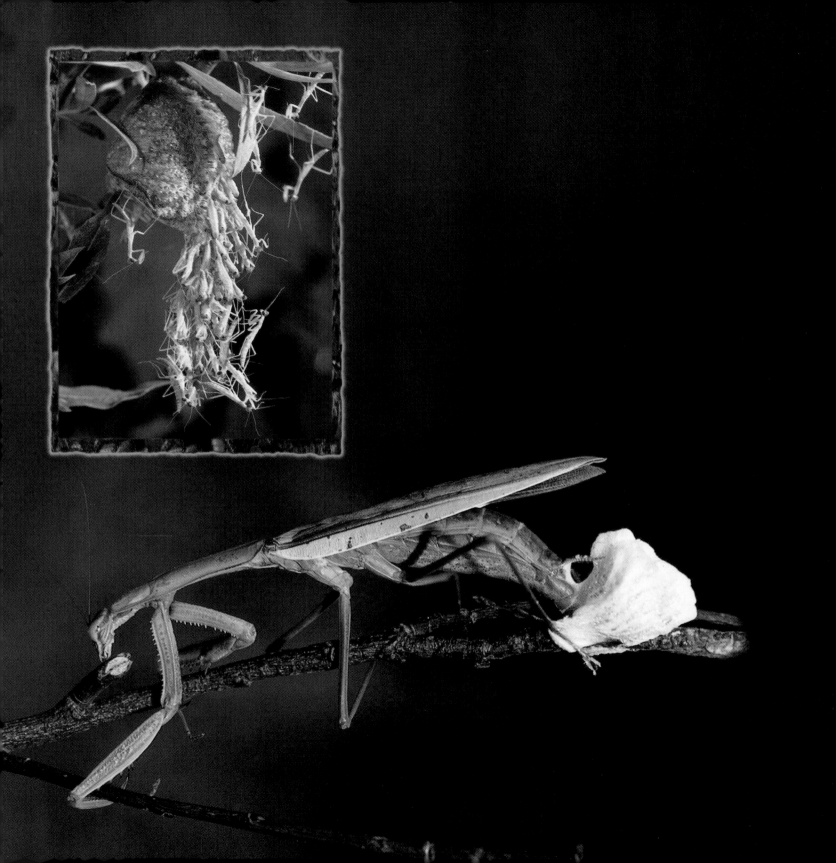

LAYING EGGS

After mating, the female mantid constructs an **ootheca**, or egg case, on a branch or a plant stem. She builds it out of a gluelike **protein** made inside her own body. The female uses the tip of her abdomen to whip the protein into a gooey, bubbly mass. She lays tens or hundreds of eggs in these pockets of air. The case hardens soon after the female completes it, making a strong home for the eggs.

A mantis might build six or more egg cases in a single season. In many mantid species, the adults die before winter. The strong, hard egg cases usually will protect their eggs until the **nymphs** hatch in the spring.

A female praying mantid builds a strong ootheca (left). Small, soft nymphs hatch from the hard egg case (inset).

HATCHING AND GROWING

When a mantid nymph is ready to hatch, its forehead swells like a balloon and splits its eggshell. The nymph tumbles out and hangs in the air by a long, thin string of **chitin**. It crawls to a branch or to the top of the egg case and waits as its **exoskeleton**, or outer shell, hardens in the open air.

As it grows, a nymph periodically **molts**, shedding its exoskeleton and growing a bigger one. With each molt the nymph grows larger. However, the basic shape of the mantid's body stays the same throughout its life. This form of development, in which young nymphs look like small, wingless adults, is called **incomplete metamorphosis**.

An orchid mantis nymph (left) will molt several times before becoming a full-grown adult with wings (right).

FUN FACTS
IN AFRICAN GRASSLANDS, WHERE FIRES MAKE THE GROUND APPEAR DARK, SOME MANTID NYMPHS CAN MOLT TO A BLACK COLOR TO BLEND IN.

HIDDEN NYMPHS

Mantid nymphs are an easy source of food for hungry insects. To protect themselves, some mantid species mimic ants, which can bite or sting their predators. Many predators have learned not to hunt ants, so they leave ant-mimic nymphs alone, too.

Orchid mantis nymphs are better mimics than are adults, whose white front wings can give them away. Some nymphs of other mantid species change color to match changes in their surroundings. In rainy seasons, when the grass is green, molting nymphs turn green. In dry seasons, when the grass and the leaves turn brown, molting nymphs often turn brown.

This mantid nymph has the dark coloring of an ant or of dry ground.

THE MYSTERIOUS KANCHONG

In 1899, a naturalist named Nelson Annandale visited Malaysia, a region of Southeast Asia. There he found an orchid mantis sitting in a flower. When Annandale asked what kind of creature it was, Malaysian people told him that the orchid mantis was very rare. They said it was not an insect, but a flower that had "come to life." They laughed when he said he would like to find another one. They said few people had ever seen more than one orchid mantis in a lifetime. Annandale and three other naturalists searched the flowers of hundreds of plants for six weeks. They never found another orchid mantis.

GLOSSARY

abdomen (AB-duh-min) The large, rear section of an insect's body.

camouflaged (KA-muh-flajd) Colored or patterned to blend into the surroundings.

chitin (KY-tin) A material that hardens to produce the hard part of insects' shells.

compound eyes (KOM-pownd EYS) The larger eyes of insects, that are made up of many simple eyes.

cryptic (KRIHP-tik) Hidden, or secret.

Eurasia (yuh-RAY-zhuh) The land from western Europe to northern Asia.

exoskeleton (ek-soh-SKEH-leh-tin) The hard outer shell of an insect's body.

incomplete metamorphosis (in-kum-PLEET meh-tuh-MOR-fuh-sis) The series of changes that an insect undergoes when it changes from nymph to adult, resulting in an increase in size but not a great change in form.

mimics (MIH-miks) Things that imitate or copy something else closely.

molts (MOHLTS) Sheds skin, feathers, or an exoskeleton.

nymphs (NIMFS) Young insects that have not yet developed into adults.

ocelli (oh-SEH-lee) Simple eyes of an insect or another invertebrate.

ootheca (oh-uh-THEE-kuh) The egg case of a mantid or a cockroach.

order (OR-dur) A group of species marked by a particular set of physical features.

pheromones (FAIR-uh-mohnz) Chemical substances used for communication within an animal species.

prophet (PRAH-fet) A person who tells the future or speaks as the voice of a god.

protein (PROH-teen) A substance found in living things that comes in many forms.

raptorial (rap-TOR-ee-uhl) Able to seize and eat living prey.

species (SPEE-sheez) A single kind of plant or animal.

thorax (THOR-aks) The middle body segment of an insect.

tropics (TRAH-piks) The warm areas on either side of the equator.

INDEX

WEB SITES

To learn more about orchid mantises, check out this Web site:
www.insecta-inspecta.com/mantids/praying/index.html